LOVE STORY FOR HER TO SMILE

S. H. WISEMAN

Love Story For Her To Smile

(Book 1)

S. H. Wiseman

love

Love is a complex and multifaceted emotion that is often described as an intense feeling of affection or attachment towards someone or something. It can be expressed and experienced in many different ways, including romantic love, familial love, platonic love, and self-love.

Romantic love is typically characterized by feelings of passion, intimacy, and commitment towards a romantic partner. It often involves physical attraction and a desire for emotional and physical closeness. Familial love, on the other hand, refers to the love and affection felt between family members, such as between parents and children or siblings. Platonic love, also known as friendship love, is characterized by feelings of affection and attachment towards friends or acquaintances. Finally, self-love involves accepting and valuing oneself, including one's strengths and weaknesses.

Love is a powerful force that can bring people together, provide comfort and support during difficult times, and enrich our lives in countless ways. However, it can also be a source of pain and heartache when relationships end or when love is not reciprocated. Despite the potential risks, many people continue to pursue love and seek out meaningful connections with others, as it is often seen as an essential part of the human experience.

Table of Contents

Chapter No # 1

A Walk on the Beach

As the sun rose over the Atlantic Ocean, Theresa Osborne stepped onto the sand in Cape Cod. She had driven all night, hopeless to escape the recollections of her failed marriage and the pain of her hubby's infidelity. The beach was cold beneath her bare bases, and the swells crashed against the reinforcement in a soothing meter.

As Theresa walked along the sand, she noticed a green bottle nestled in the beach. Curious, she picked it up and examined it. Inside was a letter, precisely folded and sealed with a kiss. Intrigued, Theresa opened the letter and read the words written on the runner.

" My Dearest Catherine," the letterbegan.However, also I'm dead," If you're reading this. But know that I've loved you with all my heart and soul. You were the light of my life, and I'll always cherish the time we spent together. Please forgive me for leaving you so soon, but know that I'll always be with you in spirit."

Theresa was moved by the words, and she could not help but wonder who this mysterious Catherine was. She felt a connection to the letter's author, as if he were speaking directly to her. She knew she had to find out further.

As she continued her walk on the sand, Theresa could not shake the feeling that commodity important had just happed to her. She had stumbled upon a communication in a bottle, a communication that had ever set up its way to her. She knew that she had to find out further about the letter's author, and she was determined to uncover the verity.

With a sense of purpose, Theresa headed back to her auto. She had a long trip ahead of her, but she was ready for whatever lay ahead. The communication in a bottle had given her a new sense of stopgap, a renewed faith in love and the power of connection. She knew that this was just the morning of a remarkable trip, one that would change her life ever.

Chapter No # 2

The Discovery

Theresa drove all the way back to her home in Boston, unfit to shake the feeling that the letter she set up was meant for her. She could not stop allowing about the man who had written it and the woman he called Catherine. Who were they? What had their story been? And how had the bottle with the letter ended up on that sand in Cape Cod?

As soon as she got home, Theresa began probing everything she could about dispatches in bottles. She read about people who had transferred dispatches into the ocean, hoping that someone would find them and write back. She read about the history of the practice, dating back centuries to mariners who would shoot dispatches to loved bones

back home. She indeed communicated a many experts on the content, hoping that they could exfoliate some light on the letter she had set up.

Days turned into weeks, and Theresa's preoccupation with the letter only grew stronger. She set up herself reading it over and over again, trying to decrypt any suggestions that might reveal the identity of the letter's author. She began to feel like she was on a hunt, one that she could not abandon until she had uncovered the verity.

One night, as Theresa sat in her living room girdled by books and papers, she entered a phone call that would change everything. It was a man named Garrett Blake, and he claimed to be the author of the letter she had set up. He'd seen an composition she had written about her hunt, and he'd honored his own words. He wanted to meet with her and tell her the full story of the communication in a bottle.

Theresa was stupefied. She could not believe that the man who had written the letter was still alive, and that he'd reached out to her. But she knew that she had to meet him. She agreed to fly out to North Carolina, where he lived, to hear his story in person.

As Theresa hung up the phone, she felt a rush of excitement and expectation. Eventually, after weeks of searching, she was going to meet the man behind the communication in a bottle. She packed her bags and headed to the field, ready for whatever lay ahead.

Chapter No # 3

Searching for Answers

As Theresa arrived in North Carolina, she felt a sense of nervous expectation. She could not believe that she was about to meet the man who had written the letter she had set up on the sand. She had so numerous questions, and she hoped that he'd be willing to answer them.

Garrett Blake saluted her warmly at the field, and she was struck by his rugged good aesthetics and easy charm. He took her to his home, a small cabin on the sand, and they sat down to talk.

Garrett explained that he'd written the letter to his woman , Catherine, after she failed in a auto accident. He'd been devastated by her loss, and he could not bear the study of noway being suitable to tell her how important he loved her. So he'd written the letter, sealed it in a bottle, and thrown it into the ocean, hoping that it would ever find its way to her.

Theresa was moved by Garrett's story, and she could see the pain and grief in his eyes as he spoke. She could also smell that there was further to the story, and she wanted to know everything.

Over the coming many days, Theresa and Garrett talked for hours on end, participating stories and recollections of their histories. Theresa set up herself drawn to Garrett, and she could not help but feel a deep connection to him. She knew that she was falling for him, and she wondered if he felt the same way.

As they sat on the sand one evening, watching the sun set over the ocean, Garrett turned to Theresa and said," I've to tell you commodity. commodity that I have been keeping from you."

Theresa's heart contended as she awaited for him to continue. She could tell that whatever he'd to say was important.

" I have been keeping tabs on the bottle," Garrett said." I have been following its trip across the ocean, trying to find out where it went."

Theresa was stupefied. She could not believe that Garrett had been searching for the bottle all this time. She wondered why he'd been so determined to find it.

" I guess I just wanted to know if it had reached her," Garrett said." I wanted to know if she had entered my communication."

Theresa could smell the pain and craving in his voice, and she reached out to take his hand. She knew that Garrett was still grieving for his woman

, and she wondered if she could ever truly contend with the memory of Catherine.

As they sat in silence, watching the swells crash against the reinforcement, Theresa knew that she had to make a decision. She had to decide whether to continue her hunt for answers, or to let go of the history and embrace the present. It was a choice that would change her life ever.

Chapter No # 4

A Surprise Encounter

Theresa couldn't stop thinking about Garrett and their time together in North Carolina. She had felt a connection with him that she had never experienced before, but she couldn't help but wonder if she was just a substitute for his late wife, Catherine. She decided to take some time to think about her feelings and what she wanted out of their relationship.

A few weeks later, Theresa received a phone call from her friend Deanna, who was visiting Cape Cod. Deanna had found a message in a bottle on the beach and was excited to share the news with Theresa.

Theresa was shocked. Could it be possible that someone had found the bottle that Garrett had thrown into the ocean all those years ago? She asked Deanna to describe the bottle and the message, and her heart raced as she listened to the details.

It was the same bottle, and the message was the same one that Garrett had written to Catherine. Theresa couldn't believe it. She felt a surge of excitement and hope, and she knew that she had to tell Garrett.

She immediately called him and shared the news. Garrett was stunned. He couldn't believe that someone had found the bottle after all these years. He asked Theresa to bring the bottle to him, and she agreed.

Theresa flew to North Carolina with the bottle in hand. When she arrived at Garrett's cottage, he was waiting for her on the porch. They hugged each other tightly, and Theresa could feel the warmth of Garrett's embrace.

Garrett took the bottle from her, and they went inside to open it. As they sat on the couch, Garrett carefully removed the note from the bottle and unfolded it. They both read the message silently, and tears filled their eyes.

"I love you, Catherine. Always and forever."

It was the same message that Garrett had written all those years ago. Theresa reached out to take Garrett's hand, and they sat in silence for a few moments, lost in their thoughts and emotions.

Finally, Garrett turned to Theresa and said, "Thank you. Thank you for finding this and bringing it to me."

Theresa smiled at him and said, "You don't have to thank me. I did it because I care about you."

Garrett looked at her with a mixture of gratitude and admiration. He knew that Theresa was a special person, and he couldn't imagine his life without her.

As they sat on the couch, holding hands and watching the sunset over the ocean, Garrett leaned over and kissed Theresa. It was a tender, sweet kiss, filled with love and hope for the future.

Theresa knew in that moment that she had found what she had been searching for all along. She had found a connection with Garrett that was deeper and more meaningful than she had ever imagined, and she was excited to see where their journey would take them next.

Chapter No # 5

A Shared Passion

Garrett and Theresa spent the coming many days exploring the strands of North Carolina, collecting seashells and ocean glass, and talking about their participated passion for jotting. Garrett was impressed by Theresa's gift and fidelity, and he set up himself opening up to her in ways he noway had ahead.

One evening, as they sat on the veranda of Garrett's cabin, belting wine and watching the stars, Theresa asked him about his jotting process. Garrett dithered for a moment, doubtful if he wanted to partake his particular studies and passions with her. But as he looked into her warm brown eyes, he felt a sense of trust and openness that he'd noway felt before.

" Well," he began, taking a deep breath," I generally start by just jotting down some notes or ideas that come to me. And also I will spend some time allowing about the characters and their provocations. Once I've a rough figure, I will start writing the first draft."

Theresa jounced, harkening hardly." And how do you stay motivated?" she asked.

Garrett signed." It's not always easy. occasionally I get wedged, and I feel like I can not write another word. But also I flash back why I love jotting, and I keep going. And occasionally, when I least anticipate it, alleviation strikes, and the words just flow."

Theresa smiled." I know what you mean. Writing is like that for me too. It's a passion that is always with me, indeed when I am not laboriously writing."

Garrett reached over and took Theresa's hand." I am so thankful that we partake this passion," he said." It's rare to find someone who truly understands what it means to be a pen."

Theresa squeezed his hand." I feel the same way," she said." And I am agitated to see where our jotting will take us, both collectively and as a couple."

Garrett leaned in and kissed her vocally." Me too," he rumored.

As they sat on the veranda , enjoying each other's company and featuring about their jotting futures, Garrett and Theresa knew that they had set up commodity special in each other. They had a participated passion that brought them together, and they were agitated to see where their trip would take them next.

Chapter No # 6

Love Notes

Theresa's daughter, Lucy, discovers a bottle on the sand containing a communication. She brings it to her mama , who recognizes Garrett's handwriting. Theresa decides to write a column about the communication and her hassle with Garrett for her review. She also writes a particular letter to Garrett, expressing her curiosity about the man who wrote the communication and her admiration for his capability to express his passions so well. Theresa prodigies if she'll ever hear back from him, but she decides to keep the possibility open by including her address in the letter.

Theresa entering a letter from Garrett. She's overjoyed and surprised that he responded to her letter. Garrett's letter is thoughtful and eloquent, and it reveals that he's a companion who lost his woman

Catherine to cancer. Garrett also shares his love for sailing and the ocean, which he inherited from his father. Theresa is moved by his words and feels a connection to him.

Theresa continues to write to Garrett, and they change letters regularly. Their letters come more intimate, and they begin to reveal further particular details about their lives. Theresa tells Garrett about her failed marriage and her fears of falling in love again, while Garrett shares his struggles with grief and the guilt he feels for moving on. Despite their differences, they both feel a deep bond and a growing magnet to each other.

As they continue to correspond, Garrett and Theresa decide to meet in person. Garrett suggests that they meet in Rodanthe, a small littoral city in North Carolina where he's restoring a sand house. Theresa agrees, and they make plans to meet in a many weeks. Theresa is agitated but also nervous about eventually meeting the man behind the love letters.

The chapter ends with Theresa's expectation and query about what their meeting will bring. She wonders if their connection will be as strong in person as it's in their letters, and if they will be suitable to overcome the obstacles that stand in their way.

Chapter no # 7

The Weekend

Theresa arrived in Rodanthe, North Carolina, feeling nervous and agitated to eventually meet Garrett. When she arrived at the sand house, he saluted her warmly, and they participated a romantic regale together. They talked about their lives and heartstrings, and Theresa felt a strong connection with Garrett. As they spent further time together, they continued to explore the city and the strands, enjoying each other's company and the beauty of the area.

Over the course of the weekend, Theresa and Garrett participated intimate moments, talking about their histories, their expedients, and their fears. Theresa felt comfortable with Garrett and was thankful for the occasion to get to know him more. As they talked, she felt a growing magnet to him and wondered if this could be the morning of a new chapter in her life.

Despite the challenges they faced, similar as the distance between them and their different cultures, Theresa felt hopeful and auspicious about their future together. She knew that there would be obstacles to overcome, but she was willing to take the threat for the possibility of love.

Their idyllic weekend was cut short when Garrett entered a call that his father had taken a turn for the worse. He'd to leave incontinently to be with his father, leaving Theresa agonized but understanding. Before he left, Garrett promised to keep in touch and told Theresa that he wanted to continue their relationship. Theresa watched as he drove down, feeling uncertain about what the future held.

As she returned home, Theresa reflected on her weekend with Garrett and wondered if their connection would be strong enough to repel the challenges ahead. She knew that there would be delicate choices to make, but she also knew that she was willing to take the threat for the possibility of love.

The chapter ends with Theresa realizing that she has fallen in love with Garrett and wondering what the future holds for them. She knows that there will be challenges and delicate choices ahead, but she also knows that she's willing to take the threat for the possibility of love. Theresa prodigies if Garrett feels the same way and hopes that they will be suitable to overcome the obstacles that stand in their way.

Chapter no # 8

A New Beginning

Chapter 8 of titled "A New Beginning," begins with Theresa Osborne reflecting on the whirlwind of emotions she's experienced since finding the mysterious message in a bottle on the beach. She's still struggling to reconcile the romantic words with the man who wrote them, and she's plagued by doubts about whether she's doing the right thing by pursuing this connection.

Despite her reservations, Theresa decides to reach out to the man who wrote the message, Garrett Blake. She's able to track him down to a small fishing village in North Carolina, where she learns that he's a widower who lives a solitary life, focusing on his work as a boat builder. When they meet, Garrett is initially hesitant to talk to her, but eventually he opens up about his late wife, Catherine, and the profound impact she had on his life.

Over the course of several conversations, Theresa and Garrett begin to form a connection, sharing stories about their lives and opening up to each other in a way they haven't with anyone else. Theresa begins to see the man behind the words in the bottle, and she's struck by his honesty and vulnerability.

As they spend more time together, Theresa and Garrett begin to realize that their connection is more than just a passing fancy. They're drawn to each other in a way that neither of them can explain, and they find themselves falling in love.

Despite their growing feelings for each other, however, Theresa and Garrett are both still haunted by the memory of Catherine. They both know that their relationship will never be able to replace what they had with their former partners, but they're willing to take a chance on each other anyway.

In the final paragraphs of the chapter, Theresa and Garrett share a quiet moment on the beach, watching the sun set over the water. As they stand together, hand in hand, Theresa realizes that she's finally found what she's been searching for all along: a new beginning, with a man who's not afraid to take a chance on love.

Chapter no # 9

A Second Chance

This chapter starts with Theresa reading the letter she found in the bottle. The letter is from a man named Garrett, and it describes his love for his wife, Catherine. Theresa is moved by the letter, and she decides to try and find Garrett.

Theresa calls the post office where the letter was sent from, and she is able to get the name and address of the person who sent it. She then sets out to find Garrett, hoping to give him a chance to explain the letter and possibly start a relationship with him.

As Theresa drives to Garrett's hometown, she reflects on her life and how she has been holding back from love. She realizes that Garrett's letter has inspired her to take a chance on love again.

When Theresa finally meets Garrett, she is struck by how much he resembles the man in the letter. They talk about the letter, and Garrett tells her about his wife, Catherine, and how she died. Garrett is still grieving, but he is also intrigued by Theresa.

The two spend the day together, exploring the town and talking about their lives. Garrett opens up to Theresa about his past, and she realizes that he is a kind and caring person who has been through a lot of pain.

As the day comes to an end, Theresa realizes that she is falling for Garrett. However, she also knows that he is still mourning his wife and may not be ready for a new relationship. She decides to give him space and time to heal.

In conclusion, Chapter 9 of is a turning point in the story. Theresa takes a chance on love and meets Garrett, the man who wrote the letter she found in the bottle. The two spend the day together, and Theresa realizes that she is falling for him. However, she also recognizes that he is still grieving and needs time to heal. This chapter sets the stage for the rest of the book and leaves the reader wondering what will happen next.

Chapter no # 10

A New Life

This chapter begins with Theresa returning home from her trip to meet Garrett. She is conflicted about her feelings for him and wonders if she should reach out to him again.

As Theresa tries to sort out her emotions, she receives a surprise visit from her son, Kevin. Kevin has been staying with his father, David, but he decided to come see his mother for a few days. Theresa is thrilled to see her son and spends as much time with him as possible.

While Kevin is visiting, Theresa receives a call from Garrett. He tells her that he wants to see her again and invites her to visit him in North Carolina. Theresa is torn between her responsibilities as a mother and her growing feelings for Garrett.

After much deliberation, Theresa decides to take a chance and visit Garrett. She arranges for Kevin to stay with his father and sets off to North Carolina.

When Theresa arrives in North Carolina, Garrett meets her at the airport. The two spend a few days together, exploring the town and getting to know each other better. Theresa is impressed by how caring and thoughtful Garrett is, and she begins to see a future with him.

As their time together comes to an end, Garrett tells Theresa that he loves her. Theresa is taken aback by his declaration, but she also realizes that she loves him too.

In the final scene of the chapter, Theresa returns home to her son, Kevin. She is filled with hope and optimism for the future, and she knows that she has a tough decision to make. She must choose between the life she has always known and the new life that awaits her with Garrett.

In conclusion, Chapter 10 is a pivotal chapter in the book. Theresa takes a chance on love and travels to North Carolina to see Garrett. They spend time together, and Garrett declares his love for her. This chapter sets the stage for the rest of the book and leaves the reader wondering what choice Theresa will make.

Second Book Is Coming Soon.

www.ingramcontent.com/pod-product-compliance
Lightning Source LLC
LaVergne TN
LVHW052104160826
845678LV00015B/3354